Famous Fables

words by Sheila Wainwright
music by Alison Hedger

A new children's musical based upon four traditional famous fables

A. Town Mouse and Country Mouse
B. Frog and Ox
C. Fox and Stork
D. Hare and Tortoise

A full performance includes acting, mime, songs (some part-work) and dance

Duration approx. 45 mins.

For children 8 to 12 years
Key Stage 2

Also suitable for performance by adults to children and family audiences

TEACHER'S BOOK
Music and Production Notes
The play is published separately GA 10976

SONGS

	1. Famous Fables	*All*
	Link song between sections.	*Or may be played by recorder*
A	2. Big Fruit Pie	*All (two parts) + mice dance*
	3. Come With Me	*Jethro and Kensington duet*
B	4. Rivers and Rivulets	*All (three parts) + frog ballet*
C	5. A Friend	*Solo Fox and Stork + dance*
D	6. A Spring in My Step	*Hare and All + Hare's dance*
		(Tortoise, Crow and All for reprise)
	7. You Can Win	*All*

A matching tape cassette of the music for rehearsals and performances is available,
Order No. GA 10977, Side A with vocals, Side B with vocals omitted

© Copyright Golden Apple Productions
A division of Chester Music Limited
8/9 Frith Street, London W1V 5TZ

Order No. GA 10975 ISBN 0-7119-4713-9

599

HISTORICAL NOTES

Fables have been associated for more than 2,000 years with the name Aesop, and can be traced back to the folk tales of the primitive peoples of India and Greece, who used them for imparting moral values. Aesop lived in Greece at around 600BC. He is reputed to have been a slave who was put to death in accordance with an oracle. He is also believed to have been "a writer of fables" though this cannot be substantiated and would seem improbable. It is probable however, that a great number of the fables associated with his name did originate through his story telling and were written down at a later date.

During the l6th Century, Jean de la Fontaine (1621–1695), from Champagne, France, became a renowned poet and was the author of a collection of some 240 poems, published in various editions between 1668 and 1694. The material for this collection was largely drawn from Aesop.

PRODUCTION NOTES

Based on four of the classic fables, FAMOUS FABLES has "hidden" lessons of life. The drama, music, dance and historic heritage all have great value, making this musical ideal for an all-year-round school production.

The work has four separate playlets linked by a theme song and/or recorder version of the song and a short introductory rhyme. FAMOUS FABLES offers approximately 45 minutes of humour and provides opportunities for a wide range of ability. There are ample non-speaking parts (mice, frogs, birds, animals, trees) and a body of singers enables those children who are off-stage, to make a valuable contribution.

A production of FAMOUS FABLES can be simple, using the bare minimum of props with little or no scenery, or elaborate with full scenery and costumes, lighting etc. just as facilities and time allow.

Any stage, large or small, traditional or in the round, or any large enough floor space (school, church or community hall) and not forgetting open air theatre, will suffice. All that is really needed is an acting area with two exits, preferably stage right/stage left. However, if necessary, one exit can work with a certain amount of ingenuity.

FAMOUS FABLES is a versatile work which can embrace the wide abilities and ages of a school. It is ideal for small groups to rehearse then come together for a performance. Alternatively, competent small groups (drama and theatre groups, single classes etc.) can give appealing and lively performances. Because of the humorous nature and scope of the work, it is expected that Upper Seniors and adult professional/amateur groups will also find FAMOUS FABLES challenging and satisfying to perform to mixed family audiences.*

The PUPIL'S play book GA 10976 has the characters, props, etc. listed for each section. Please refer to this for casting.

MUSIC

FAMOUS FABLES will appeal to anyone who likes a tuneful melody. Children will eagerly learn the music and the songs provide opportunities for part singing. The off-stage choir plays an important role giving musical support to those on stage.

The piano part has been kept fairly simple and chord symbols are given. Please feel free to embellish the accompaniment as desired. The music will orchestrate well if needed.

DANCES

These can be performed as simple action routines or choreographed in a classical manner. The Frog Ballet in particular will give the children an opportunity to work out a humorous routine — much leaping and popping about is envisaged!

Both Sheila Wainwright and Alison Hedger hope that the happy time spent creating FAMOUS FABLES will be contagious, making your performance an enjoyable experience for participants and audiences alike.

* A minimum group of 5 adult players is required, with some doubling of parts. The performance will be slicker and be approximately 30 minutes.

1 (i)
FAMOUS FABLES

All
Song opens musical and is repeated between each section.

With gentle movement ♩ = 120

1. Fa - mous fa - bles, tales from the past. An - cient leg - ends with mor - als that last. Fa - mous fa - bles, these you may know. Time - less sto - ries from long a - go.

2. We bring you pearls __ of wis-dom so true, hid-den in col-our-ful
3. Les-sons in life, full of hu-mour and guile. Light-en your hearts and be

tales just for you.
rea-dy to smile.

Fa-mous fa - bles, these you may know.

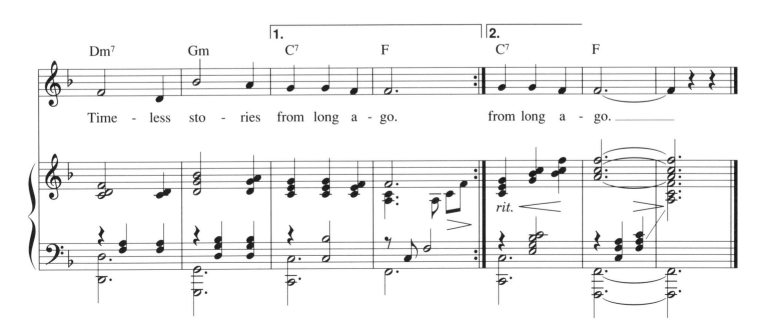

Time - less sto - ries from long a - go.

from long a - go. __

(ii)

FAMOUS FABLES

Recorder. An alternative version of Song 1.
To be played between each section

BIG FRUIT PIE

All (two parts) + mice dance

repeat as necessary

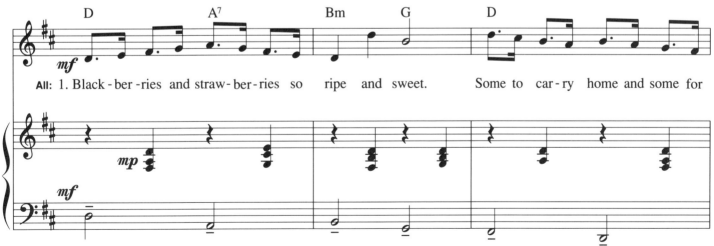

All: 1. Black-ber-ries and straw-ber-ries so ripe and sweet. Some to car-ry home and some for

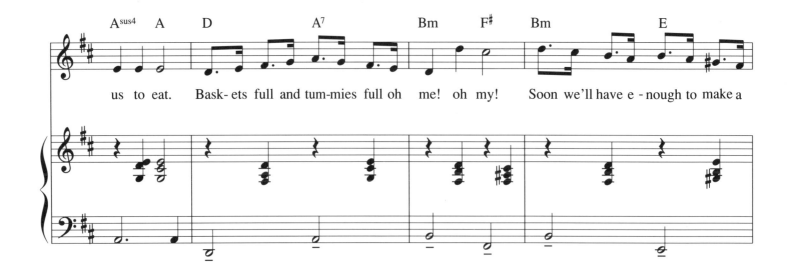

us to eat. Bask-ets full and tum-mies full oh me! oh my! Soon we'll have e-nough to make a

Chorus

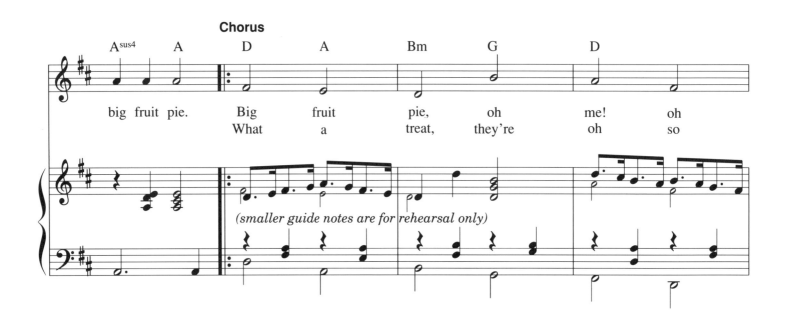

big fruit pie. Big fruit pie, oh me! oh
What a treat, oh they're oh so

(smaller guide notes are for rehearsal only)

my! Soon we'll have a big fruit
sweet. Save the best and eat the

8

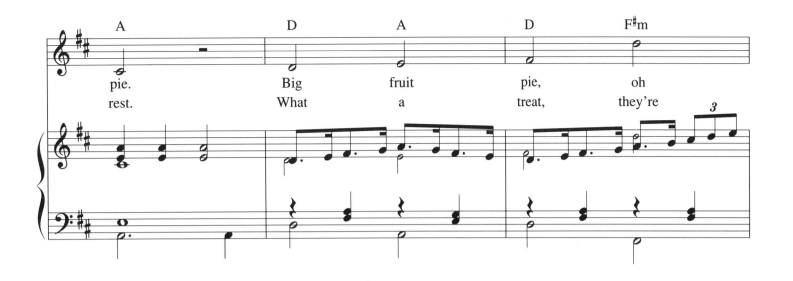

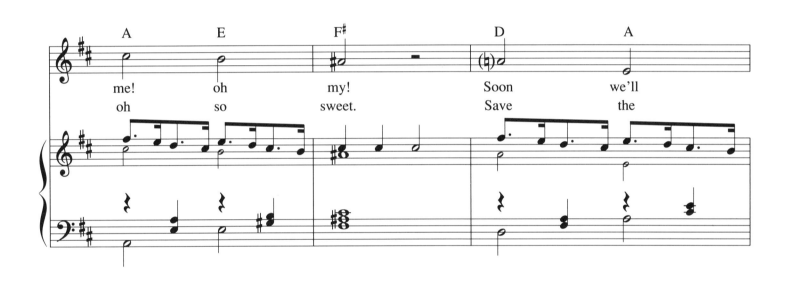

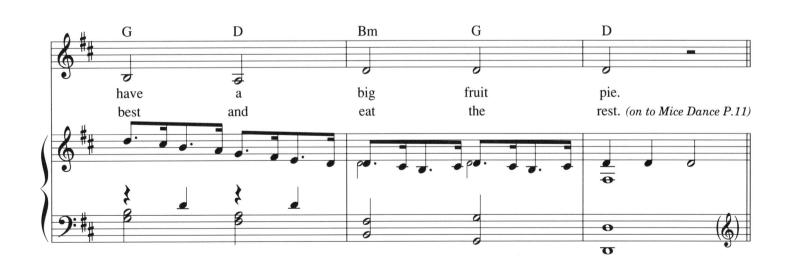

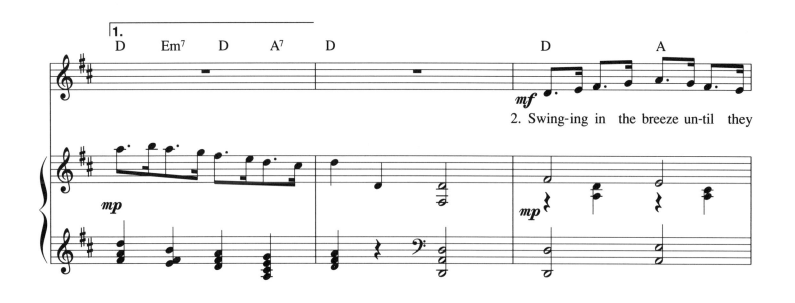

2. Swing-ing in the breeze un-til they

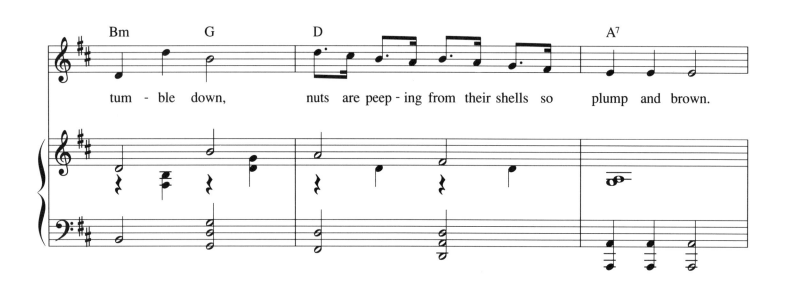

tum - ble down, nuts are peep - ing from their shells so plump and brown.

Mun - chy and crunch-y and oh so sweet. Save the best and eat the rest! Oh what a treat.

MICE DANCE

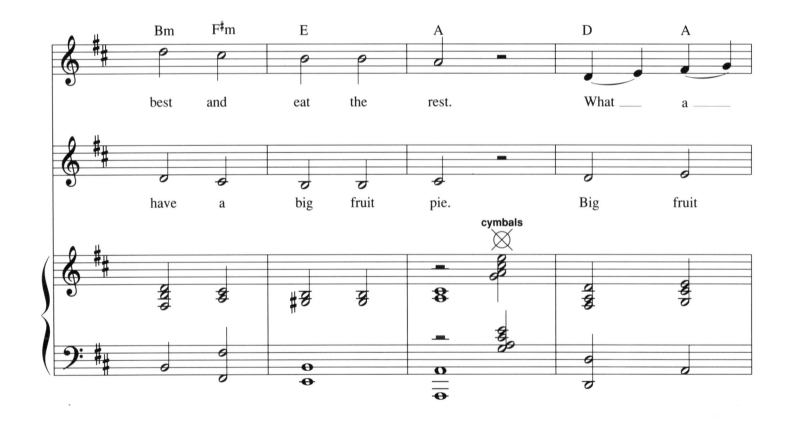

treat, they're oh so _____ sweet. Save _____ the _____

pie, oh me! oh my! Soon we'll

cymbals

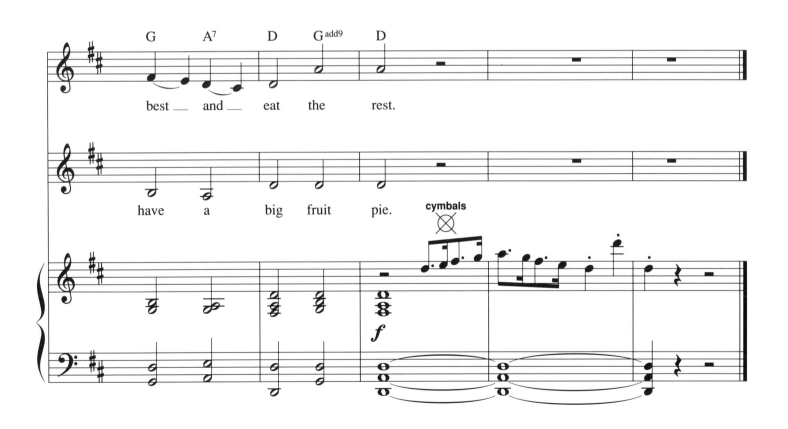

best _____ and _____ eat the rest.

have a big fruit pie.

cymbals

3 (i)

COME WITH ME

Jethro and Kensington
Cue: Come with me to the city . . .

Jauntily ♩ = 120

Kensington:
1. Come with me, mon cher a - mi,___ Let me take you on a___ spree.___ The
2. Come a - long with me, mon_ cher,___ Where there's 'chic' and 'sa - voir - faire'.___ It's

1.
at - mos - phere is full of_ fizz.___ Trains go ZOOM and street - cars_ WHIZ!

razz - le - dazz - le, style and flash. Come with me, let's make a dash.

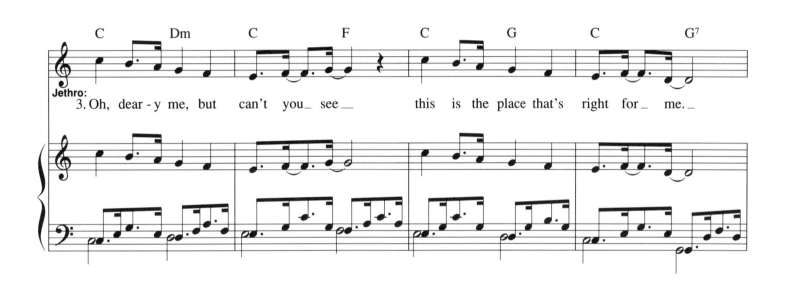

Jethro:

3. Oh, dear - y me, but can't you see this is the place that's right for me.

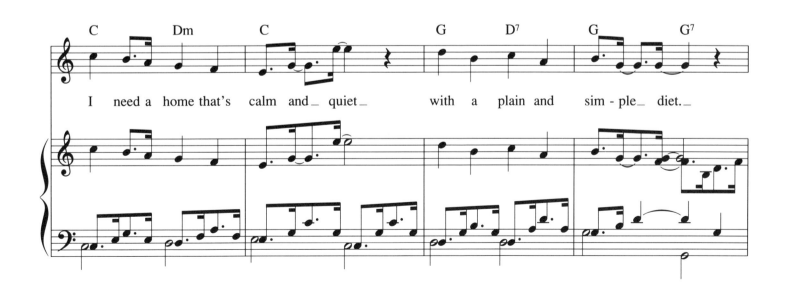

I need a home that's calm and quiet with a plain and sim - ple diet.

4. Dine with me on can - a - pés, __ cakes and cham - pagne ev - ery __ day. __

Jethro:
Though it's tempt - ing I a - gree, __ it's not quite the life for __ me. __

16

Duet

Kensington: Come with me, mon cher a - mi. ___ Let me take you

Jethro: Oh, dear-y me, but can't you ___ see ___ this is the place that's

mf

on a ___ spree. ___ The at - mos - phere is full of ___ fizz. ___

right for ___ me. ___ I need a home that's calm and ___ quiet ___

Trains go ZOOM and street - cars ___ WHIZ! ___ Dine with me on

with a plain and sim - ple ___ diet. ___ Dine with ___ you on

17

can - a - pés,___ cakes and cham - pagne ev - ery___ day.___

can - a - pés,___ cakes and cham - pagne ev - ery___ day?___

Why not try it? Come and __ stay. Off we go then, ___

_____ (nods) _____ Off we go then, ___

lead the __ way! __

lead the __ way! __

18

3 (ii)

COME WITH ME

Jethro
Cue: Didn't I tell you I'd show you excitement old fella, eh?

Lyrics: Jethro: Come with me, my dear old friend to a place where we can spend happy days in peace and quiet, where we'll eat a

simple diet. You can keep your noise and dash,

razzle-dazzle, style and flash. Give me a safe and

gentle, sentimental,

country life!

B

Introduction
FROG BALLET

(dancing continues during song Chorus)

Full of fun ♩ = 184

Frogs: Pop, pop, pop, pop, bub-ble, bub-ble, pop. Pop, pop, pop, pop,

L.H. 8ves for repeat

bub-ble, bub-ble, pop. POP!!

Straight into Song 4

21

4
RIVERS AND RIVULETS

All (three parts) + frog dancing continues during Chorus
Also SONG REPRISE
Cue: No . . . we never heard a thing!

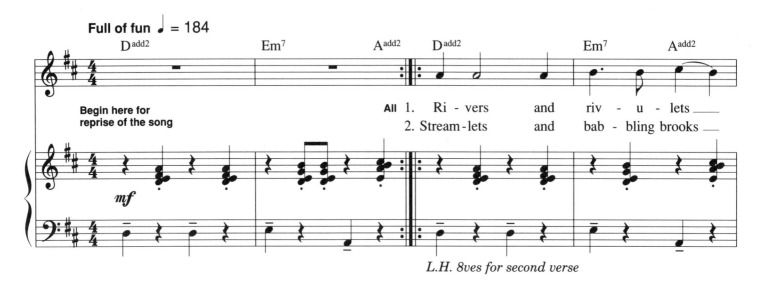

Begin here for reprise of the song

All 1. Ri - vers and riv - u - lets _____
2. Stream-lets and bab - bling brooks _____

L.H. 8ves for second verse

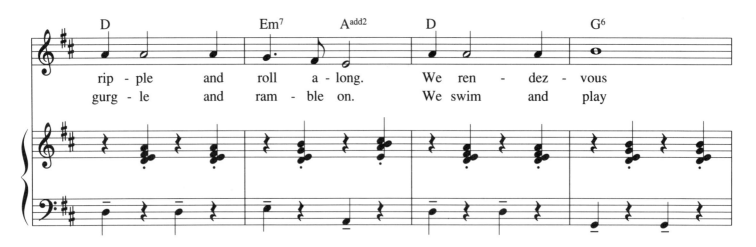

rip - ple and roll a - long. We ren - dez - vous
gurg - le and ram - ble on. We swim and play

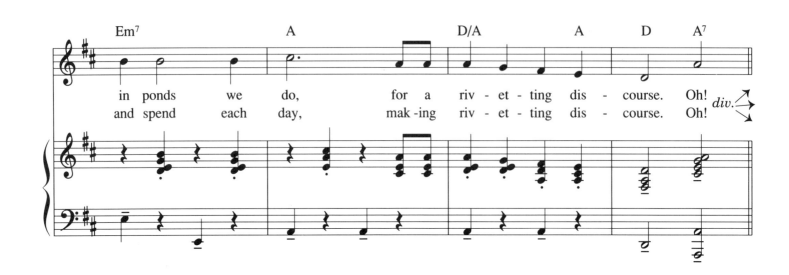

in ponds we do, for a riv - et - ting dis - course. Oh!
and spend each day, mak-ing riv - et - ting dis - course. Oh!

div.

Chorus (frogs dance during Chorus)

OPENING MUSIC

A FRIEND

Fox and Stork + dance
Cue: . . . likeable guest for so special an occasion . . .

DANCE

Change to Stork's kitchen

MUSICAL INTERLUDE

Stork: La, la, la, la, la, la, la, la   *etc. (or humming)* . . . .

Knock at door as piano plays last note.

5 (ii)

A FRIEND

Cue: A little . . . beef stew . . . music?

D

A SPRING IN MY STEP

Hare and All + Hare's dance

mead-ows and the trees all the birds and the bees_ have been out and a-bout since

dawn - ing.__ 2. What a sea - son for fun__ and fol - ly.__ There's no

rea - son for blues,__ be jol - ly.__ Now that win-ter is o - ver__ let's

roll in the clo - ver, 'cos__ SPRING HAS SPRUNG! SPRUNG!

7 i)

YOU CAN WIN

All
Cue: Get a move on lazybones!

win. Stay right on track and nev - er look back, keep go - ing and don't give in.
win. The win-ning post is near if you keep on go - ing and nev - er fear.

Keep on — go - ing, don't look back. You can — win!

1.
2. Animals exit and trees enter and take positions for 'woodland scene'.

You can win . . . You can

whispering

win . . . You can win . . . You can win.

35

MUSIC FOR FOREST ANIMALS' DANCE

Cue: . . . before I go and collect my prize! (Hare falls asleep)

Repeat as necessary, until all trees have made their exit.

YOU CAN WIN

All
Cue: . . . as we wait for the winner to arrive . . . Caww!

6 REPRISE

A SPRING IN MY STEP

Tortoise, Crow and All
Cue: But I thought . . . How on earth?

meadows and the trees all the birds and the bees have been out and about since dawning. 2. What a season for fun and folly. There's no reason for blues, be jolly. Now that winter is over let's roll in the clover, 'cos SPRING HAS SPRUNG! SPRUNG!

Animals:

Printed and bound in Great Britain by
Caligraving Limited Thetford Norfolk